HARLEY-DAVIDSON 45s

WORKHORSE AND WARHORSE

HARLEY-DAVIDSON 45s

WORKHORSE AND WARHORSE

John Carroll and
Garry Stuart

OSPREY
AUTOMOTIVE

First published in Great Britain in 1994
by Osprey, an imprint of Reed Consumer
Books Limited, Michelin House,
81 Fulham Road, London SW3 6RB and
Auckland, Melbourne, Singapore and Toronto.

ISBN 1 85532 444 X

Project editor Shaun Barrington
Editor Julia North
Page design Paul Kime/Ward Peacock
Partnership

Produced by Mandarin Offset
Printed in Hong Kong

Half title page
*The US Army WLAs were fitted with
blackout lights, a partially shielded
sidelight, a standard army blackout
lamp alongside the horn and the main
headlamp, which was often painted
olive drab*

Title page
*The heavy duty luggage rack and
brown leather saddlebags were
specifically ordered for the US Army.
The rack was intended to be strong
enough to carry a radio. The twin
military taillights were fitted on WLAs
from 1942 onwards*

For a catalogue of all books published by Osprey Automotive
please write to:

**The Marketing Department, Reed Consumer Books,
1st Floor, Michelin House, 81 Fulham Road, London SW3 6RB**

Introduction

Harley-Davidson have been making motorcycles in Milwaukee, Wisconsin since 1903. Some of their recent advertising rightfully points out that the company has survived a number of wars, a depression, foreign competition and even a Marlon Brando movie. It is against this background that they manufactured and sold the 750cc sidevalve as both a two- and three-wheeler for more than forty years. The economic and political fortunes of America are reflected far more in the mid-sized 45 sidevalve than in the bigger and more glamorous models. The Knucklehead, Panhead and Shovelhead might have been the bikes that grabbed the headlines, but the smaller capacity sidevalve was always in production, powering working bikes and trikes, carrying soldiers, policemen and garage mechanics. The one area where the 45 did grab the headlines was racing; it was the Harley 45 that provided the competition for the main rival, Indian's racers. Out of these race bikes eventually came the Sportster, a motorcycle that is still in production.

Max Middelbosch's museum in Zwolle, Holland. The two 45 race machines have Triumph gearboxes and Hunt magnetos to improve performance

Contents

It's somehow appropriate that even Uncle Sam rides a 45 – the Harley that has carried America's soldiers, policemen and workers across four decades

Depression

The Forty-Five, as it is known because of its displacement of 45 cubic inches, debuted in 1928, for the 1929 sales season, at a price of $290. The new model was typical of American bikes of the time with a solo saddle, footboards, a long tank and valanced mudguards. Production commenced in July 1928 but got off to a slow start. Engineering problems were partially to blame – the earliest models were prone to shearing the woodruff key that positioned the sprocket on the gearbox countershaft. This was quickly solved by using a larger key and correspondingly enlarged keyway. The first 45 models were known as the Model D and had a 4.3:1 compression ratio, a 0.75" venturi and a 32 tooth rear sprocket. In September '28 the DL appeared with an increased specification: a 5:1 compression ratio, 0.875" venturi and 28 tooth sprocket. Most of the engineering problems had been solved by December 1928. The clutch was redesigned the following year to incorporate 14 springs instead of 12, and the asbestos friction discs were riveted on. Until then it was similar to those fitted to Harley's single cylinder bikes. In the 1929 line up were F-head big twins, sidevalve and overhead valve singles and the sidevalve 45s. It was the latter model that created most interest and was compared to Indian's 101 Scout. Partisan Indian riders often referred to the Harley 45 as the 'three cylinder Harley' because of the vertical positioning of the generator at the front of the engine. One problem that was experienced with some Harley-Davidson 45s was caused by the primary and final drive chain being on opposite sides of the bike and the gearbox being solidly bolted to the frame. It resulted in sufficient torque loading being applied to the frame to twist it out of alignment. A model designed for sidecar work was designated the DS. It came with a 4.3:1 compression ratio, and a 36 tooth rear sprocket geared the bike to pull the extra weight of a sidecar. Developmental problems such as those described led to the cessation of 45 production in the spring of 1929. The infamous Wall Street Crash of that year, when share prices fell dramatically, heralded the beginnings of the Great Depression. Subsequently, the selling of motorcycles became exceptionally difficult for American manufacturers throughout the thirties. However, the sidevalve concept had caught on and Harley's big news for 1930 was that sidevalve 74 cu in big twins replaced F-heads in the line up for that year, although sales of bikes naturally began to drop off soon after the Wall Street Crash.

The 45 was reintroduced for 1930 with a new frame and new front fork

Above

The 45 sidevalve debuted in 1928 with the Model D and was quickly followed by the DL, the DLD and the DS. This DL dates from 1930 and is on display in Max Middlebosch's Zwolle, Holland motorcycle museum

Right

The DL was sometimes referred to as the 'three cylinder Harley' because of the vertical positioning of the generator in front of the front cylinder

assembly. Saddle height was lowered by 2.5" but ground clearance was increased! A criticism of the early 45s had been that they grounded while cornering. The new forks were I-beam section forgings but still of a springer design. The primary chain was lubricated by a line which led directly from the oil pump, while the clutch was enlarged to the same size as big twin ones. A handclutch lever was available as an option.

The DLD was a sports model with 6:1 compression ratio, 28 tooth sprocket and a large carburettor; 1.25" as opposed to the 1" fitted to the D, DS and DL models. The standard finish was olive green but other colours were available on special order through dealers. The 1930 model 45 retained the vertical generator but has the look of the later 45s with valanced mudguards, springer forks, hand gear shift, a steel primary cover, rear stand and solo saddle. Despite the Depression, Harley-Davidson sold 6,222 45s in 1929 and 4,946 in 1930 – out of total production of 20,946

The DL was a more sporting version of the Model D and came with a 5:1 compression ratio instead of the 4.3:1 of the D and DS. The DLD had a 6:1 compression ratio and produced approximately 20 hp @ 4000rpm

The twin headlamp arrangement seen here was superseded by a single 7" diameter headlamp for 1931 onwards, although the fork mounted toolbox remained

and 17,662 for those years - giving false hope before the economic disaster.

In 1931 the 45 was upgraded in terms of both styling and engineering details. Stylistic changes consisted of a new single headlamp, fork mounted toolbox, horn and new handlebars. Engineering changes included the fitting of the bigger brake from the 1929 F-head big twin, a gear lock to stop the transmission from jumping out of gear, a new silencer and a diecast Schebler carb.

After engine number 31D1786 in September 1930, a new generator drive was incorporated on the DLD and a redesigned clutch, incorporating a different sprocket, inner roller race and bearing washers, key ring and outer plate as well as extra steel friction plates. Other modifications included new valve spring covers, a crankcase breather pipe and oil pump (the primary chain oiler now came straight out of the oil pump body).

Tom Sifton, the Harley dealer for San Jose, California, went to the Milwaukee factory in July 1931 to collect the first 1932 45 model. William S. Harley asked Sifton what he thought of the 45 sidevalves and what problems he'd experienced with them. Sifton revealed that he had to weld a reinforcing bar to each frame before selling the bike. William S. Harley ordered the factory to weld a similar strut onto the frame of the new bike and all new 45s until a stronger component could be incorporated into the frames. The 1932 45 retailed for $295 at the factory. The Depression worsened, resulting in pay cuts at the factory and a drop in sales – especially overseas. The company planned to build only 9000 bikes and in December 1931 Walter Davidson was considering whether the company had a future of any sort. A small capacity single cylinder bike that had been discontinued some years earlier was reintroduced at the cheap price of $195 to attempt to boost sales. The 45 went into the 1932 catalogue in a further refined form – it became the Model R. A major change was the mounting of the generator horizontally across the front of the engine, and the front frame downtube was bowed slightly to make sufficient room. The RL and RLD were sporting models while the RS was the sidecar model. The engine used larger flywheels which necessitated larger crankcases; inside were magnesium alloy pistons with gudgeon pin circlips and chrome vanadium steel piston rings. The conrods were lengthened and the little ends had bronze bushes. Stronger valve springs, an improved crankcase breather and a new oil pump were all incorporated. The latter item could now be removed from the engine without removing the timing gear cover. The frame was made from heavier gauge tubing and stronger forgings while the forks were correspondingly strengthened. Of the 9000 planned bikes, only 6841 were produced, including 110 for the US Army and 2000 exported. Due to the precarious state of the company few changes were made to the 45 for 1933, although later in the year diecast Linkert carbs took the place of the Schebler components that

had been used for the past couple of years. The 'buddy seat' became available as an option, as did the front fork 'ride control'. America was in the depths of the Great Depression, and it was not a good year for Harley-Davidson – they sold only 3,703 motorcycles.

Further improvements were made to the 45 for 1934 – a redesigned oil pump and aluminium pistons were incorporated into the engine. After engine number 34R4000 the cylinders were straight bored; until then they had been taper bored because they distorted to the correct shape as they became heated. A 12 spring clutch, as on the 74 cu in twins, was introduced into the transmission. The frames and forks were heat treated to make them stronger. A rear mudguard with a streamlined taillight was used for this year only. A front stand was available, but tended to be fitted to bikes destined for export; chrome plating was available as an extra cost option. The 1934 models were on sale in many cases for as long as sixteen months due to the amount of stock in dealers showrooms, but during this period 10,000 bikes were sold; this was a definite improvement over the previous year. In 1935 the factory continued using straight bore cylinders and elliptical t-slot pistons, and upgraded the quality of steel in the

Above
In 1932 the Model D range were superseded by the R, RL and RLD models. The R, as this 1933 model shows, retained the low compression ratio but was significantly improved internally, including the use of aluminium pistons in place of Lynite ones

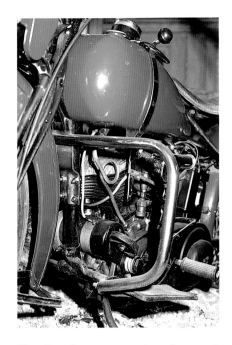

The 45 underwent a number of external changes for 1932 including the repositioning of the generator. As can be seen on this 1933 Model R it was now horizontally mounted across the front of the engine where it would stay for the remainder of 45 production

crankpins. A few other changes were made, including the introduction of a constant mesh transmission on solo models, a quickly detachable rear wheel, a new rear brake and a hub driven speedo. The RLDR debuted for hillclimbing and racing in Class C.

Whilst the really big news from Harley-Davidson for 1936 was the introduction of the 61 cu in ohv EL 'Knucklehead' powered motorcycle and the first ohv V-twin from Harley Davidson, more changes were announced for both the engine and the cycle parts of the 45. The number of cylinder head bolts was increased by one to eight on each cylinder and larger fins were included in the redesign to increase cooling. A 'Y' shaped inlet manifold was fitted and on both RL and RLD models the diameter was increased to 1.25" while the carburettor venturi was increased to 1.0625". The frame was slightly redesigned to improve handling by reducing the fork rake by 2 degrees and trail by 0.5". Use of a fork spring shield was instituted and this remained a standard fitting on 45s until 1939. The brakes were upgraded with thicker shoes being installed, the chainguard was extended and better oil seals were fitted to the gearbox. The factory looked into the subject of accessories and offered 'standard' and 'deluxe' accessory groups across the range. On the 45 the standard group comprised a safety guard, a jiffy stand, an illuminated speedo face, a ride control and a steering damper. The Deluxe group consisted of chrome plated parts, a mudguard lamp stoplight, a dice gearshift knob, saddlebags and hangers, and dice that covered the switch keys.

In 1937 the 45 models were redesignated as the W-series, while the larger 74 and 80 cu in sidevalves became known as the U-series. Along with this came new 3.5 gallon tanks to give the look of the 61 cu in ohv models right across the range. The 45 gained a ride control with the adjuster on the left to enable the rider to easily adjust it while riding without having to release the throttle. Various engineering details were improved; the transmission gearshaft main bearings were changed to roller bearings and the cam gears were now one piece. New crankpins with one oil passage were fitted as part of a redesign of the lubrication system which also included a new oil pump. The pump had a vane oil feed and gear scavenge. Horizontal cooling fins were cast into the left crankcase and the timing cover. Harley's racer, the WLDR, had 1.3125" inlet valves while the other 45s retained the 1.25" diameter ones. The Accessory groups varied for 1937 but included such items as pedal rubbers, licence plate frames and conchoed saddlebags.

After the success of the overhead valve 61 cu in model, Harley-Davidson investigated the viability of an ohv 45 cu in motorcycle. A prototype based around the basics of the 45 sidevalve was constructed and the directors discussed the project for some months, but it never went into production.

The spring of 1937 saw a couple of events that, while not affecting the

production of the 45 cu in sidevalve models, did affect the company as a whole. The first of these was the unionisation of the workforce in March, and this was followed by the death of William A. Davidson on April 21st. He was the Vice-President of the Company and the first of the four founders to pass away.

For 1938 the major improvement to the 45 was made to the transmission. Most visible was the fitment of a big-twin style underslung rocking clutch pedal. The clutch was strengthened by the use of an eight ball thrust bearing in place of the six ball one. Inside the gearbox a slotted drum shifter cam, similar to those on the larger capacity bikes, was installed. New synthetic oil seals helped reduce oil leakage and around the bikes could be found new grease nipples to make them compatible with garage greasing equipment.

In 1939 the 45 transmission was upgraded with the use of needle roller bearings. This replaced the bronze bushing fitted on the kickstarter side of the countershaft gear. A new washer and a redesigned bush increased the oil flow into the clutch gear bearing. Tall finned alloy cylinder heads debuted on the 1940 WLD; there was 51.5% more cooling area. This allowed much faster dissipation of heat, and the heads were 8 lbs 2 ozs lighter than the iron ones. Harley believed that faster cooling equated with longer engine life, and promoted this benefit in their advertising. Tubular springer forks were fitted to the 45 for the first time.

Another minor improvement was implemented in 1941 when valve springs 0.625" longer were fitted to prolong valve spring life. The compression ratio on WLs with iron cylinder heads was reduced to 4.75:1 from 5:1. The Servicar compression ratio was increased from 4.5:1 to 4.75:1 in order to simplify the spares situation.

These changes meant that all 45 sidevalve iron heads were now the same. A major redesign of the clutch took place; the release lever was strengthened and given a larger pushrod bearing. The clutch was equipped with two fibre discs and one spring disc giving a total of six friction surfaces; the friction material was riveted to the discs. The spring load was decreased from 500 to 300 lbs and a larger hub was fitted and held in place with splines rather than a key and keyway. All this contributed to smoothing out the clutch action. Inside the gearbox the gears were strengthened and increased in diameter. Shifting gears was made easier by the fitment of a redesigned cam and shifter lever. Three studs now held the gearbox to the frame and the filler was relocated. These were the last fundamental changes to be made to the 45 transmission and made it

The 45 was upgraded in numerous details throughout the thirties, despite the Depression. Exports helped to keep the company in business; this RL was sold in Holland

almost 0.5" wider. A new brake drum with 44% greater surface area for better braking and longer brake lining life was fitted to the back wheel. The teardrop shaped toolbox was fitted for the first time to the 45.

Above

For the 1935 sales year the 45 engine gained straight bore cylinders and elliptical t-slot pistons in place of the taper bore cylinders and round pistons. The reason that both components were not round was to allow for the expansion of the metal as the engine became hot

Right

The streamlined taillight, as seen on this RL, was available only for 1934 although many '34 bikes were on sale for up to sixteen months as a result of low sales during the Depression

War

In November 1938 William S. Harley suggested to the other Directors that the company seek military business in view of the Government's increased defence spending. He went to Washington D.C. to investigate the possibilities and then went on to a motorcycle reliability conference at Camp Holabird, Baltimore, that had been called by the Quartermaster Corps. During the conference he received an order for 2000 motorcycles. Military business wasn't new to Harley; they'd supplied large numbers of machines for use in the First World War. In the early thirties Harley-Davidson sidecar outfits were used by the US Navy as emergency fire tenders at Floyd Bennett airport in New Jersey. The Governments of countries to which Harley exported were also interested in the Milwaukee bikes for military use. For example, in 1939, the Dutch army used Harley-Davidsons – this included machine gun equipped sidecar outfits.

On July 1st 1939 the total strength of the US Army numbered approximately 175,000 men. Of these, 75% were spread across the United States in over 130 camps, stations and posts. The remaining 25% were overseas. Corps HQs existed more in an administrative rather than tactical way. There were, on paper, nine Infantry Divisions but only the 1st, 2nd and 3rd had the framework of a divisional organisation. The 1st and 2nd Cavalry Divisions were both in excess of 1,200 men short and poorly equipped. The only mechanised brigade was the famous 7th Cavalry. Lack of motor transport made training difficult. Later the same month, the army was permitted an increase in size to 210,000, essentially to increase the size of the Panama Garrison and The Army Air Corps.

The first two prototype WLA 45s for the Army were finished in August 1939 and sent to the Armoured School of the Mechanised Cavalry Board at Fort Knox – more usually known for its role as the US bullion

Right
"Harold Holdem of Troop A. 1st Reconnaissance Squadron. He is equipped with a Thompson submachine gun used for the protection of despatch rider carrying confidential messages from Army Headquarters to the Field Command during recent manoeuvres of the First Cavalry Division of US Army". This was the original caption to the picture. Contrary to the impression given by this photograph taken in the USA, the 1st Cavalry Division was not mechanised. The 45 here appears to be a basic late thirties model. Note the valanced mudguards and chrome trim. (Imperial War Museum)

depository. They were essentially civilian WLs painted gloss green and retaining vestiges of civilian trim in the form of chromed headlamp surrounds, white twistgrips and beehive taillights – albeit painted. Rectangular footboards were fitted as were 'I' section forks.

World War Two started on September 1st 1939, when Germany invaded Poland. On September 8th, President Roosevelt declared a limited National Emergency because of the war in Europe, and raised the strength of the Army to 227,000. The National Guard was also permitted to recruit significant numbers. These recruiting drives allowed the General Staff to establish several tactical corps HQs and enough troops to create a fully

Above

Cpl. R. Power with the Canadian Provost Corps is seen checking a driver of a military vehicle for his driving licence and work ticket. The Canadian Provost Corps has many jobs to do, patrolling roads and giving assistance to soldiers and civilians. This is a 1942 WLC. Note that it has no luggage rack. (Imperial War Museum)

Right

A Canadian motorcyclist finds himself the centre of interest in the grounds of an English country house that was used as a brigade HQ. This WLC is fitted with a pillion seat, something that WLAs were not equipped with. The passenger footrests take the place of the rear crashbar. (Imperial War Museum)

Special squads of motorbike troops are trained at a US Camp in Australia. This rider reportedly "tore up to position at 35mph, leapt off and was in action with Tommy gun in 3 seconds". The military taillights fitted to WLAs from 1942 onwards can be clearly seen. (Imperial War Museum)

functioning field army. General Marshall, who had been appointed Chief of Staff on September 1st 1939, ordered a basic reorganisation of the infantry division. This involved reorganising the 3.5 existing but incomplete four regiment 'square' Divisions into five smaller, three-regiment 'triangular' Divisions. The intention was to make the infantry more manoeuvrable and more flexible. This was tested in April 1940 when the first proper Corps manoeuvres since 1918 were held. Then, in May, Corps-v-Corps exercises including the first tests of new weapons and tactics were held. Some emergency expenditure was permitted including $12,000,000 to purchase much needed motor transport, including motorcycles. Mechanisation of the Cavalry had begun in 1936, but been hampered by a lack of funds.

The reorganisation also intended that non-divisional cavalry, in the form of cavalry recce Squadrons, was intended to ride 'point' ahead of the new divisions. A Squadron consisted of three Recce Troops and nine Recce Platoons. They were to be transported in a variety of motor transport including White Scout cars, M3A1 Dodge 4x4 Command cars and Harley-Davidson 45 motorcycles. There would be eight solos and three sidecar outfits in each Troop. Unlike the German Army, who used sidecar outfits as mobile machine gun platforms, the intention was that motorcycle borne soldiers would be employed for dismounted scouting.

The staff of Fort Knox had begun a programme of testing machines from Indian, Delco and Harley-Davidson soon after the outbreak of war in Europe. Much of the testing was done at low speeds in order to gauge the

Snowdrops (MPs) police US Army in Britain. A squad of men of the Traffic Control Section sitting astride their motorcycles outside Headquarters before going on duty. The bikes are standard 1942. (Imperial War Museum)

running temperatures of the engines although the machines had to be capable of 65 mph. The fact that the Army was testing military motorcycles more than two years prior to the US involvement in the war perhaps indicates the inevitability of the US fighting with the Allies. The results of the tests were interesting as various aspects of each machine were praised and criticised. The Delco (a machine similar to a BMW) was in many ways considered superior to the Indians and Harleys as it was shaft driven, had telescopic forks, considerable ground clearance and was light in weight. The army testers liked the Indian's left hand throttle because it allowed riders to use their right hand for traffic signalling and convoy duties. The Harley seemed to fare better in fording rivers, and the greater clearance between its tyres and mudguards led to less problems on muddy tracks. On the other hand, the Harleys did suffer as a result of water ingression into the primary case and damage to the primary chain and clutch.

In March 1940 Harley-Davidson received an order for 745 of its WLA models, presumably to equip the new Recce Squadrons. The bikes were essentially the prototypes that had been tested, although they had the tubular forks as newly fitted to the civilian models. The forks were 2.375" longer than standard to increase ground clearance. The 1940 WLAs were fitted with buddy seats, luggage racks and D-shaped floorboards. A further US Army order for 659 motorcycles followed.

Harley produced variants of its military bikes for export throughout 1941. In this year significant numbers of military WLs, known as WLCs,

were built for Canada, one of the Dominions that had come to Britain's aid. In 1940 a contract to supply South Africa, another of Britain's Dominions, with 2,056 motorcycles and 156 sidecars was also signed. Later in the year, Harley-Davidson received orders from the British War Department for 5000 machines following the destruction of the Coventry Triumph factory, amongst others, during the blitz of November 1940.

1941 WLA models were equipped with the cylindrical oil bath air filter mounted on the left side of the bike behind the rider's leg. This was retrofitted to earlier army 45s. WLAs for this year also had a buddy seat, a civilian '34-38 rear lamp with a single blackout lamp mounted above it and a modified civilian luggage rack. They had a semi-circle cut out to allow the rear portion of the mudguard to hinge up without the extra

Above
Pfc Carl Sturdevant, one of the motorcycle escorts who helped to escort convoys through London. The wartime censor has obliterated part of the unit marking on the front mudguard. Note the painted headlamp. (Imperial War Museum)

Left
Pt Jacob Zuideme and Pfc William Foster, two of the motorcycle escorts who helped convoys through London. Although the Harleys are standard 1942 US Army WLAs, they do not have the ammunition box and scabbard on the front forks like those used in combat areas. (Imperial War Museum)

light interfering with the rack. The new clutch release arm and teardrop toolbox were also fitted. The WLCs for 1941 differed in some respects from the WLAs. Most of them did not have the cargo rack on the rear mudguard. The front brake was the same as used on the big twins which was fitted to the hub with lug screws; front and rear wheels were interchangeable. An auxiliary hand clutch lever was fitted to the right handlebar. A front stand was fitted to the mudguard in the same manner as the rear one and a toolbox was fitted to the front mudguard; Canadian military blackout lamps were fitted front and rear. Some WLCs had pillion seats which were referred to as 'tandem' seats; where these were fitted, the rear crashbar was not fitted and passenger footrests were bolted to the frame tubes. By June 1941, Harley-Davidson were finding it difficult to get materials for production of anything other than defence – involvement in the war in Europe was looking inevitable and steel and aluminium were in short supply. Domestic orders were dispatched to dealers slowly to maintain their businesses.

The WLDR was discontinued in the Autumn of 1941 and the WR was dropped in December. The new sales brochure produced in late 1941 for the '42 sales season reflected the uncertainty of the times; it read, 'We have all had days of trial in the past and we have come out on top. We will do so again'.

The Japanese airstrike against Pearl Harbour on December 7th initiated the United States' entry into the Second World War. At this time the US Army numbered 1,686,000 men in 29 Infantry, 5 Armoured and 2 Cavalry Divisions. Mobilisation continued apace, and by 1942 a further 65 Divisions were activated. The increase in size of the Army required a further reorganisation which took place on March 9th 1942, and the trend towards mechanisation quickened. In January 1942 the company had won a contract for 31,393 motorcycles which were to be finished by the end of December 1943. This contract was to provide the majority of Harley-Davidson's wartime business. The profit per bike was to be 6% before taxes. At the beginning of February civilian production was abandoned for the duration of hostilities. On February 7th Walter Davidson died; he was the second of the founders to pass away. William H. Davidson was elected to his position in the management of the company.

Vibration, especially during use on surfaced roads, proved something of a problem, so heavier frame castings were used and a stronger rack and rear stand were fitted. On WLAs the twin rear lamp set up was instituted.

Despite the cancellation of civilian production, export contracts for military bikes were still being fulfilled at a fast rate. In March 1942 Harley-Davidson received another order from South Africa, this time for 1622 sidecar outfits. In May, deliveries of the 45s ordered under the new contract started and from June onwards the bikes were supplied in

Right
Rough riding US Army military police toughen up on practice riding pits in Britain for the tougher job ahead, to prevent supplies and men piling up confusion on beach heads when the Allied attack on Nazi-held Europe starts. (Imperial War Museum)

Below right
Lieutenant Howard T. Chase briefs US Army motorcycle military police before they take off for a day's manoeuvres on their obstacle course; it is in preparation for vital policing duties when Allied troops hit the beach heads of Europe. (Imperial War Museum)

accordance with the uprated and improved 1942 specifications.

By 1942, when it became the engine of the US military motorcycle in large numbers, the 45 cu in sidevalve engine had been considerably refined from the one that was introduced in 1928. The 45 degree V-twin engine had a bore of 2.75" and a stroke of 3.8125", giving the displacement of 45.12 cu in. It had a compression ratio of 5:1 and developed 23 bhp at 4600 rpm. An engine unit retailed at $155. The crankshaft consisted of two flywheel halves which combined the functions of crank throws, flywheels and counter weights were connected by a steel crankpin. This assembly was arranged so that both pistons moved in the same direction at the same time. One cylinder would be on the exhaust stroke when the other was on the compression stroke. Both conrod and

Above

Originally the US Army intended to use eight solo motorcycles and three sidecar outfits as part of recce squadrons to ride point ahead of the Armoured Divisions. Brian and Skilly of the UK HD 45 Owners' Club have restored this WLA as a machine of the 2nd Armoured Division. The sidecar is not the original

Left

A motorcycle rider of only two months, Pvt. Wilburn L. Cummings flies high over a shell hole obstacle course somewhere in England. The course is designed to acquaint riders with conditions similar to those they expect to face under combat. (Imperial War Museum)

crankshaft main bearings were rollers. The crankshaft was housed in two cases, and one case also formed the timing gear case. This contained four gear driven tappet cams, one of which drove the generator, the ignition circuit breaker, oil feed pump, oil scavenge pump and the crankcase breather valve. The breather valve was the only connection between the two cases and provided a way for the oil to leave the crankcase and enter the gear case. The conrods were of the yoke type and the forked rod went into the rear cylinder. The pistons were made from aluminium and tapered 0.003" towards the skirt. They were ground elliptical in shape with the longer dimension, by approximately 0.030", running from front to rear of the engine. The purpose of this was because of the way the components distorted as they became heated. The pistons would fit tightly in the bores when cold and yet would expand sideways along the gudgeon pins as they warmed up, thereby not damaging the engine. Each piston had two compression rings and one oil control ring. They were available in oversizes to allow for rebuilds in plus 0.010" intervals to a maximum of plus 0.070". Pistons above plus 0.030" had t-slots machined in them to allow for excessive expansion when hot. The cylinders were made of cast iron and the valve seats were cast into the barrels. Exhaust valves were made from higher grade steel than the inlet ones because they had to operate at much higher temperatures. The Army WLA and WLC models had aluminium cylinder heads. The engine was of a dry sump design, the oil tank held 7 pints of oil that was force fed to the engine bearings by a vane type pump mounted on the outside of the gear case cover. The oil pump was gravity fed and the oil was returned to the tank by a gear-type scavenge pump. The Linkert carburettor was gravity fed from the 3.33 gallon tank and mixed with the air at an approximate ratio of 13:1 – air to petrol by weight. Ignition was wasted spark through using a circuit breaker rather than a distributor. The air filter was of an oil bath type. Use of this was instituted when it was discovered that many army motorcycles were suffering engine failures due to dirt getting into the combustion chambers in cross country use. The standard air cleaner, which on a motorcycle was near the ground, was unable to cope with the dust created, and the particles that were ingested subjected the piston rings and cylinder bores to a lot of wear resulting in a lack of compression. The throttle was on the right handlebar grip and the ignition advance/retard on the left. There had been experiments with left hand throttles especially on police bikes.

By June '42 Harley were turning out 750 bikes per week for Army, Navy and Canadian contracts. This figure receded to 675 in August as material shortages made themselves felt. The specification of the WLA was changed slightly, and from June onwards the slightly shorter civilian forks were again fitted despite reducing the ground clearance. A Linkert

Because of the scale of recruiting for and mechanisation of the US Army for its involvement in World War II, huge numbers of motorcycles were purchased. This necessitated the training of both rider and mechanics; cut-away engines such as this were used as teaching aids

John McKenna from Fayettville, New York, proudly displays the WLA that he owns – it came from the US Army and had been stored unused for almost 40 years

M88 carb with a fixed high speed jet and a smaller venturi was used, the purpose of which was to stop riders from 'adjusting' the carb themselves, reportedly a major cause of breakdowns on Army bikes. On '42 WLA and WLC models the headlamp was moved down lower and closer to the mudguard than on early civilian bikes to reduce the chances of it being smashed when the bike was dropped. Also fitted were parts designed to further protect the bike during off road use and crashes, namely crashbars front and rear. A range of standardised military parts were incorporated including taillights, sump guards, blackout front lamps and oil bath aircleaners. A circular one was fitted on '40/41 bikes while a square version of these were fitted from 1942 onwards. Both types were made by The Oakes Product Division. Other parts exclusive to the military were part numbers 11201-M and 11202-M, an ammunition box and a scabbard carrier for either a rifle or a machine gun.

Windshields, legshields and protective canvas aprons were also fitted to military 45s, but tended to be used only in winter months. They were progressively redesigned throughout the war.

In the Autumn of '42, the Army requested that Harley slow their production of the bikes to be supplied under their contract to 345 motorcycles per week. Harley maintained this level for the next fourteen months but because of other contracts such as those for WLCs actually averaged approximately 475 motorcycles per week. The company also turned its Milwaukee factory service school into a Quartermaster School for military mechanics.

Harley-Davidson's own magazine, *The Enthusiast*, which dates back to 1916 and is still published, took a patriotic look at military Harley riders in their wartime issues. In December 1942 the magazine reported on numerous civilian motorcyclists who had joined up, as well as the motorcycles that Harley-Davidson had supplied to the US forces. Fort Knox was featured as the largest motorcycle mechanics school in the US and part of the Armoured Force School, and by then already had 10,000 mechanics pass courses there in the nine depots.

Camp Roberts in California, a US Army Replacement Training Centre (RTC), was also reported on. The purpose of an RTC was to provide a steady flow of trained men to tactical units, thus relieving them of training duties during mobilisation and combat. During hostilities the RTCs had two requirements to fulfil: firstly to supply filler replacements in units being activated or brought up to strength, and secondly to provide loss-replacements for units engaged in combat that suffered casualties. At Camp Roberts it was the MPs who used WLAs for road patrols around the camp, traffic direction, convoy duties and regulation of military vehicles.

Material shortages were likely to affect motorcycle production; rubber was in short supply as a result of the Japanese conquests in Asia. Ways of

saving rubber were investigated and explains why early military 45s have the traditional Harley bicycle pedal kickstarter, while later ones have a single metal tube type.

On May 12th 1943, Harley-Davidson were presented with the first of three Army-Navy E for Excellence awards. The award and a banner were presented to Company President William H. Davidson by Colonel C. J. Otjen of the US Army who described Davidson's workers as 'the soldiers of the production line'.

In the August 1943 issue of *The Enthusiast*, the spotlighted military riders were tagged the 'Rough Riders of Camp Carson'. They were in fact the Reconnaissance Troop of the 89th Infantry Division who were then training at Camp Carson in Colorado. The Rolling-W, as the 89th were nicknamed, went on to take part in the liberation of Europe and won battle honours at Bigen and Eisenach. It is worth noting that the

Above
Claudia Perry from New York riding the 1942 WLA that she bought as a rough non-runner in 1990. She is a member of the American organisation, the Military Vehicle Preservation Association. Her bike is painted as one that was used in England during WWII

Right
An owner riding his WLA in the rain at an English Harley rally. His bike is equipped with all the kit a US soldier would have carried

Reconnaissance Troop who rode their WLAs across extreme terrain recommended a tyre pressure of 8 psi for off road use.

Throughout World War Two, Lend-Lease Harleys were supplied to the Armies of both the USSR and China. The USSR used them, including sidecar outfits tagged WSRs, in its fight against the Germans. The WSR was a WLA motorcycle with a very basic sidecar on the right hand side. The Chinese made use of WLAs in their fight against the Japanese. These were not the first Harleys used by the Chinese Army – they had used a number of VL outfits during the campaigns against the Japanese in Manchuria during the thirties. Incidentally, the Japanese also used Harley-Davidsons in the same campaigns, both the Milwaukee products and Rikuo Type 97 copies of the VL.

A retired Indian Army Major, J. C. Cross, related an amusing anecdote to the author about one particular Lend Lease WLA intended for Chiang Kai-shek. Large amounts of military hardware and vehicles, including Harley-Davidson WLAs, were being supplied to Chiang Kai-shek's forces to assist in the fight against the Japanese. Much of this equipment was being delivered over the Ledo Road which led from Assam across the Brahmaputra River at Gauhati, alongside the railway to Ledo, into and over the Patkai Mountains to Burma. Along this route were located various military units including mobile workshop units whose job was to keep all the military traffic moving. Vehicles that broke down were recovered to one of these workshops. One such was 53 Mobile Workshop under the command of Captain Charles Boynton. A Harley 45 outfit arrived in need of repairs in order for it to be delivered to the Chinese forces. While BSA and Norton motorcycles were common among units of the British and Indian Armies, Harley-Davidsons were not. The bike created such great interest among those who could ride a motorcycle that someone decided to 'liberate' it.

The soldier charged with delivering it was dispatched on the pretext that it would take a long time to get the necessary spare parts, thus leaving the bike in the hands of the workshop. The Harley, soon repaired, became something of a toy for the officers and soldiers stationed in Gauhati including James Cross, then a Captain, commanding 28 Motor Ambulance Section. He recalls teaching an Indian Havildar (Sergeant) to ride from the sidecar. The Indian was aboard the motorcycle and had gained the basics of operating the machine but not all the subtleties of steering it, allowing for the peculiar handling characteristics of a sidecar outfit. As he attempted to turn a corner on the track he began to lose control. The instructor jumped out as the outfit lifted a wheel and with the Havildar still aboard left the track, careered down a bank and into a small lake. Fortunately there were no injuries beyond hurt pride, and the sidecar was winched from the water and put back into use. It remained in

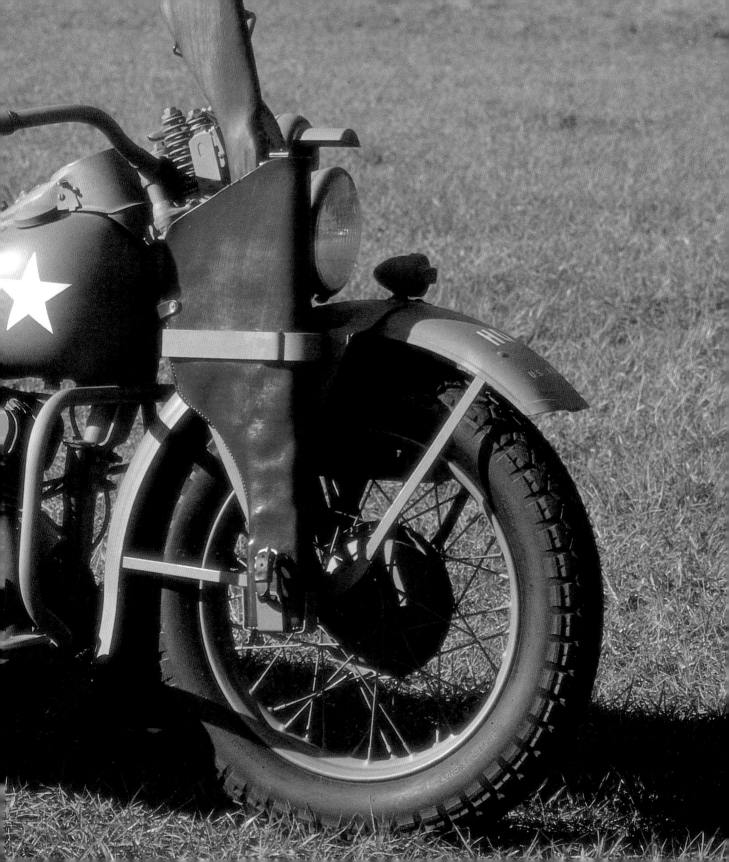

Left

The data plates fitted to the tank of WLAs varied from year to year – the 1942 models had this one made from brass. Previously they had been made from copper, and when these materials became scarce in 1943, they were made from steel

Above

The data plate was redesigned for 1944, being enlarged in the process. A space was provided for the bike's serial number and date of delivery

Gauhati when Captain Cross was posted elsewhere six months later.

On September 18th 1943 William S. Harley died – he was the third of the company's founders to do so. In November of the same year the Army cancelled an order for 1,105 motorcycles. Cutbacks in military contracts continued in 1944 when the Army realised it had sufficient motorcycles. It is worth remembering that the years of the Second World War had seen the US Army change from being reliant on horses to being totally reliant on motor vehicles. Vehicles like the Jeep had been enormously successful and had relegated the motorcycle to a service machine, the mount of Military Policemen and convoy escorts.

The '44 WLAs were different from their predecessors in a number of respects. A more basic front mudguard was one of the most obvious changes. A pressed steel elbow for the carburettor air intake took the place of the cast alloy item. Radio suppression equipment was fitted, and after 42WLA60000, an enlarged data plate was bolted to the dash. By late 1944 the war was, in the main, going in favour of the allies in both the Pacific and European Theatres of Operations. Germany capitulated in May 1945, Japan surrendered in August and all incomplete military contracts were

cancelled. Through the war years, Harley-Davidson had produced 88,000 motorcycles and copious amounts of spares.

The US Marine Corps used a variety of motorcycles, including the larger capacity Harley UA model flatheads and Indians, as well as 45s. There is documented use of bikes by The USMC in New Zealand, The Philippines, Washington, Camp Pendleton, Northern Ireland, Iceland, Wake Island and Camp Elliot in California. In the main their use was for garrison duty, delivering messages, and shore patrol.

Above

The WLC was fitted with different rear lights from the WLA, these blackout lamps were specified by the Canadian Army

Left

Alan Dark, a member of the British Military Vehicle Trust, from Swansea in South Wales, restored this WLC from a number of boxes of parts. It is painted as a US Army bike and ridden regularly to and from military vehicle meets

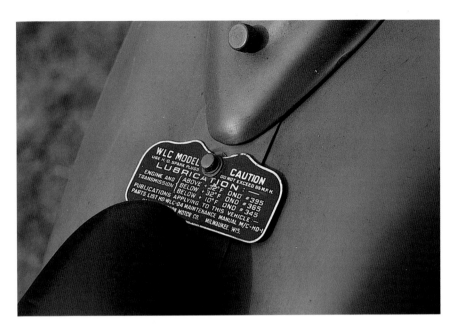

Above

The WLC also had a data plate on the tank; this one is the plate as fitted to '42-43 WLCs and contains lubrication information

Right

A Sergeant riding a 1942 WLC through a ford 'somewhere in England' during a training exercise for despatch riders. Behind him is a corporal on a BSA M20. They are followed by another WLC. (National Motor Museum)

Above

French Army returns to France. A motorcycle unit of the French Army waits for embarkation orders near the docks in an English seaport town. Allied craft transported them across the English Channel to fight on French soil for the freedom of their homeland. Summer 1944. (Imperial War Museum)

Right

Although the liberation of Europe was yet to start, the Allies finally conquered the Axis forces in North Africa in 1943 after the Battle of Kasserine Pass. Here, General Von Arnim is taken into captivity by the British watched by a curious American MP on a 1942 WLA. The end of the fighting meant that the XA would never be required by the army in large numbers. (Imperial War Museum)

Overleaf

August 1944: Americans, including a large group of military policemen, on standard 1942 WLAs embarking for France at Berth 107 in Southampton Docks. (Southampton City Museums)

Above

The RAF moves up to the Front in France. The convoy about to leave Creully, north west of Caen. July 1944; a WLC in use by the RAF; note handclutch and rider holding bike on the front brake. (Imperial War Museum)

Left

Military Police direct traffic to Coutances. Sergeant Joseph A. De Marco (left) of New York City gets information from American military police stationed at a crossroad at Les Champs de Losque, France in the drive to Coutances. The number on the front mudguard, which has been partially obliterated by the wartime censor, indicates that this WLA belongs to the 1st Army. The obliterated part would have indicated the division and regiment to which the motorcycle belonged. Coutances was liberated in July 1944. (Imperial War Museum)

Experimentation

Parallel to the supply of the WLA and WLC models to the allied forces, Harley-Davidson experimented with another design of motorcycle at the request of the US Government. They had looked closely at the motorcycles of the Axis forces who used significant numbers in their blitzkrieg style of warfare. Perceived as advantages were telescopic forks, shaft drive, rear suspension and cooler running engines. The army were looking at both solo motorcycles and trikes and wished to incorporate some of the new features into these vehicles. They wanted shaft drive bikes because it did away with chain drive and necessity for continual adjustment.

In order to familiarise the company with the European-style machines, William S. Harley purchased a BMW from a source in Holland during 1939. Harley had to compete against both Indian and Delco for military business and all three companies had supplied experimental machines for evaluation – Indian their militarised Sport Scout, and Harley the military specification WL as described. Delco provided a machine that was basically a BMW copy. The Army was still interested in shaft drive bikes and issued a specification for a motorcycle that was similar to the military BMW.

Approximately a year later a meeting was held at Camp Holabird, Baltimore, to discuss shaft drive motorcycles. William S. Harley attended on behalf of The Harley-Davidson Motor Company and was asked to bid on various types of shaft drive motorcycles. After some deliberation he agreed to bid on a basic BMW-style machine. In February 1941, Harley presented the Army with varying prices for their XA model depending on how many were ordered. The Army ordered 1000 at a unit price of $870.35, to be delivered by July 1942.

The XA was essentially a copy of the BMW R12/R75 series and so had a horizontally opposed twin engine. Bore and stroke were both 3.0625" and gave a capacity of 738 cc or 45 cu in, a displacement more commonly associated with the sidevalve V-twin. Valve actuation was by means of a single camshaft positioned in the crankcase and running in bronze bushes. The crankshaft was a double-throw item so the motion of each piston and con rod was equal and opposite. The main bearings were ball bearings. This ensured that the engine was in almost perfect mechanical balance. The con rods were two piece items with removable end caps that ran on roller bearings. The XA featured wet sump lubrication and the oil was circulated by a camshaft end, worm gear driven pump in the bottom of

Peter Maas from Helmond, Holland found this 1942 XA in parts at an autojumble and painstakingly rebuilt it with parts sourced from several countries

The XA was constructed at the request of the US Government. Harley-Davidson received a contract for 1000 of the flat twin machines

the crankcase. The crankcase held four pints of oil and breathed by means of a timed rotary device driven from the camshaft drive gear. The cylinders were exposed to the airstream as the machine was ridden and therefore operated at lower temperatures than the V-twins, something that is reported to have had a beneficial effect on the longevity of the engine. This and the fact that the machine had 'double-decker' cooling fins meant that it ran around 100 Fahrenheit degrees cooler than the V-twins – something that would have been beneficial in the North African campaigns. (The campaign in that area was over before the XA was ready for frontline operation.) The army discovered, in testing, that the XA engine lasted between ten and fifteen thousand miles before needing a major overhaul. The air cleaner was a standard military oil-bath canister type reflecting the machine's likely use in dusty conditions. The configuration of the engine necessitated twin carbs. The bike returned approximately 35 mpg.

The cycle and transmission parts of the XA also differed from Harley's more usual motorcycles. The transmission was four speed and gearchanges were accomplished with a 1 down, 3 up foot shifter on the left side of the bike. The driveshaft ran down the right hand side of the bike from the gearbox to the rear hub. The clutch lever was handlebar mounted and operated by the rider's right hand. A transmission mounted lever allowed the rider to quickly select neutral. The kickstarter was transversely mounted; to kick the engine over, the rider stood facing the left side of the machine and kicked the lever downwards. The throttle was on the left handlebar grip and the front brake lever was adjacent.

The frame was a tubular cradle type with plunger rear suspension and, up front, Harley fitted their springer forks although they were 1.5" longer than stock WLA ones. Around this HD fitted as many of their stock parts and as much of the standardised US military equipment as necessary; the rear lights, blackout sidelight, Thompson machine gun scabbard and holder, crashbars and military windscreen. Some parts had to be modified to fit, such as the back mudguard and the luggage rack which had to be kept shorter at the sides in order to accommodate the plunger suspension. Correspondingly short saddlebags were manufactured to clear the exhausts. The XA in this form weighed 565 lbs and had a payload of between 250 and 300 lbs.

The first XA sent to the army was rigorously tested at Camp Holabird, Baltimore, in the months from December '41 to February '42. After doing more than 6000 miles the XA had burned a valve, broken a gear housing and broken the prop shaft cushion flange. This latter failure was of no consequence because it was a mock up flange made from bronze because the production cast iron items weren't ready in time to be used on the pilot models. The US Army, who were also testing Indian's 841 shaft drive

transverse V-twin, deferred a decision on a major order until all 1000 XAs were supplied. They were delivered by July 1942. The Army still hadn't made its decision by March 1943 although there was talk of orders for 25,000 bikes of either the Harley-Davidson XA or the Indian 841 depending on which was chosen.

The December 1942 issue of *The Enthusiast* shows pictures of XA models in use at Camp Roberts in California and at Fort Knox. At the latter camp there is a photo of no less a person than Lieutenant John E. Harley, the son of one of the company's founders, on an XA. An Editor's note points out that the model is experimental, built at the request of the US Army, and that it was impossible to say what effect this may have on future designs.

Harley-Davidson, in conjunction with other US manufacturers such as Allis Chalmers, looked into the use of the XA engine as the power unit

The flat twin was closely based on the BMW machines used by the German Army. It displaced 45 cu in like the WLA engine but was noted for running considerably cooler – something that would be an advantage in hot climates

The XA was the first Harley-Davidson to have rear suspension, and the only Harley to date to have shaft drive. Both these features were inspired by the German BMW and Zundapp motorcycles

for both snowmobiles and generators. In July 1943 the Army Ordnance Department advised HD that the XA had been dropped from Army plans and that the WLA 45 cu in motorcycle would remain the standard US Army motorcycle. Harley immediately sought to recover the costs of tooling and development of the XA from the Government. It's no surprise that the XA was dropped; the war had moved on so far from when the XA project had been conceived with the end of hostilities in North Africa. The light, four-wheel-drive Willys Jeep had in the main relegated the Motorcycle to rear areas and to a tool of the Military Police, so bikes were required in much smaller numbers. Only this initial batch of 1000 XAs were produced and they were still officially in the experimental stage in 1943. Of the 1000, 800 were distributed among units of the Armoured Force for general testing and experimentation. Harley-Davidson's publication *The Enthusiast,* for December 1942, shows pictures of XAs in use at Camp Roberts in California and Fort Knox. It is believed that the XA never saw combat although some apocryphal tales have made it into print claiming that they did. A full XA maintenance schedule appears in the 1943 publication – Motorcycle Mechanics Handbook, The Armoured School Motorcycle Dept, Fort Knox, which perhaps indicates how close the XA came to being ordered in large numbers for the US Army.

The XS was an XA with a sidecar fitted, it never really went beyond the experimental stage. The XS had a driven sidecar wheel and Firestone 5.50x16 tractor-type tyres for greater cross-country ability, but the US Army preferred the 4x4 Jeep. The sidecar wheel was driven by means of a ring and pinion arrangement. Another experimental XA was one fitted with 5.50x16 tyres aimed at giving the bike greater capability in sand; another had a type of telescopic fork.

A large number of parts were unique to the XA – even parts which look as though they are common with the WL series. The fuel tank, seat, luggage rack, rear mudguard and so on look similar at a glance, but are in fact different. The 42XA also has a number of firsts to its credit: the first footshift Harley-Davidson, the first Harley with rear suspension, the only Boxer twin they've ever made, the only shaft drive they have ever made to date and the first Harley to have a frame number.

Above

The XA has a number of the standard US Army parts fitted including the military lights, scabbard bracket and ammunition box. Many of the other parts such as the rack are exclusive to the XA

Right

Peter Maas riding his XA. He regularly rides it to shows, and at one Harley Owner's Group event was presented with a Trophy by Willie G. Davidson, a grandson of the founders

Winning the Peace

War surplus sales were a boon to the company. In the US, dealers sold military 45s as a stop gap until civilian models became plentiful again. Harley-Davidson resumed full civilian production in 1947 as materials became more widely available. Around the world army surplus 45s made cheap, rugged transportation and no doubt did much to popularise the marque. The Harley-Davidson Riders' Club of Great Britain was formed in 1948, and amongst the founders was dealer Fred Warr. Although Warr's of London had been Harley-Davidson dealers since 1924, it was the cheap and plentiful 45s that enabled many British motorcyclists to buy Harleys. It was the same in other countries too – in Holland new civilian models went on sale immediately after the war but army surplus machines provided cheaper transport for both private and commercial users. There had, for example, been a number of Harley Clubs in Holland before the war – The Harley-Davidson Club of The Hague being one. One of the oldest clubs still in existence is the Harley-Davidson Club-Utrecht which was formed on 31st March 1962. Later it changed its name to HDC-Nederland.

Left

A 45 from 1945 which has been restored in civilian trim. It's likely that this is one of the bikes that Harley-Davidson would have made for military contracts that were cancelled towards the end of the war

Right

The 45 in standard military form had aluminium cylinder heads and a 5:1 compression ratio. In this form it produced 23 bhp at 4600 rpm

The Dutch roadside repair service, the ANWB, started up again after the war with its road patrols mounted on 25 ex-Canadian Army WLCs. Seven were adapted to take sidecars built by Hollandia, and started rescuing broken down motorists on April 15th 1946. They worked from the cities of The Hague, Rotterdam, Amsterdam and Utrecht. The number of dilapidated vehicles on postwar roads meant that the Wegenwacht, or Roadwatch, patrols were soon busy and more outfits were required. However there was a scarcity of materials for sidecar construction, so huge metal boxes made from recycled airdrop canisters were installed to seven 45s. Into these were cleverly packed a toolkit, spare fuel and oil, warning flags and so on. The weight of such a trunk made riding the Harleys difficult, especially in windy conditions. Despite this, the Wegenwacht rescued many motorists and the ANWB stayed with Harley-Davidson sidecar outfits when funds became available to buy new machines.

There were even Harley clubs on the far side of the 'Iron Curtain' in Poland, Hungary and Czechoslovakia, for example. The reason for this was the same as the clubs in the free world; because of the war, surplus Harleys were available. In this case members rode lend-lease machines left behind by the Russian Armies. Due to the 'cold war' politics, the Polish club was cut off from supplies of spare parts and new machines and its members remained mounted entirely on WLAs, known as 'Voolas', until the 1980s. Following the break-up of the Soviet Union the situation has of course altered. It was a similar story in Czechoslovakia which, before the war, had been an export market for Harley-Davidson – indeed there was a Prague Harley Club founded in 1928 – but another club was formed in 1963 by six army surplus WLA owners, The Harley-Davidson Club, Brno. The communist government registered the club members for openly liking American products, monitored their travel and generally harassed them. Despite this, the club had around 40 members by the time of the dissolution of the communist regime.

In India, an unusual vehicle appeared. It was based around the 45 sidevalve, and called a Tempo. Military bikes were left behind by the various armies and services who had been based there. Many of them were locally converted to something resembling a Servicar. A suitable car axle was installed after being converted to chain drive and an extraordinarily large body capable of seating six people was bolted over the axle. The Tempo, painted in bright colours, would then operate on fixed routes around cities such as Delhi, stopping anywhere for fares as long as there was a spare seat. In recent years the hard-worked sidevalve engines, worn out and devoid of spares, have in the main been replaced with industrial diesel engines installed in the Harley frames.

In America, production of new civilian sidevalves continued apace. Production of the WLA continued, too, for military customers, and

Above

John Luzietti, from Cocoa in Florida, is seen here riding the civilianised 45 in the spring sunshine. The wide handlebars are mounted on risers to give an upright riding position

Right

In Holland, Harley 45s are known as Liberators, a name which reflects their role in World War II. Ben Donders has rebuilt this Liberator as a civilian model with copious amounts of chrome

endured into the 1950s. The military-style rear luggage rack was offered as an accessory for riders who required a heavy duty rear luggage rack – it is listed in the 1947 official Accessory Catalogue. Also listed are numerous parts for owners to upgrade their 45 to suit both taste and pocket. A hand clutch lever for 45 solos, part number 2555 38 for '38-41 45 models and 2555-41A for '41 onwards cost $7. A range of stands: front rear and jiffy were all available as extras. Harley offered special tools for their 45s too; for example, part number 17032-X – a spoke nipple wrench $1.20. They offered exchange Linkert carburettors and a range of parts which they considered gave 45s a 'safer, smoother' ride. A steering damper was $3.30, a hydraulic shock absorber $14.75 and an adjustable ride control $7.25. Police equipment was also available for 45s including part number 11225-37, a rear wheel siren for 45 solos for $37.50 and 11225-31, a front wheel siren for Servicars for the same price.

On July 4th 1947, during the AMA races at Hollister, things got a little out of hand. It was this incident and the subsequent media exaggeration, including the movie 'The Wild One', starring Marlon Brando, that created the myth of motorcyclists as folk-devils. While the riders were not seen exclusively on Harley 45s the style of the bikes, known as Bobbers, certainly set the trend for the future. A Bobber was a Harley or an Indian with all the excess parts removed to make it lighter – this also rendered it faster. The mudguards were shortened and racing style seats and other components used. The term chopper also originated here, as riders 'chopped' off all the surplus parts.

In November 1947 Harley-Davidson announced, for the 1948 sales season, the Panhead – big news indeed. The Panhead, so nicknamed because its rocker covers looked like inverted cooking pans, was an overhead valve model and replaced the Knucklehead in Harley's line up. In Germany, sales of new Harleys, including the 45 sidevalves, started again in 1949 through an importer based in Aachen, and a new catalogue was published for that year.

The traditional workaday sidevalve 45 reached the end of the road as a solo motorcycle in 1952. In its place Harley-Davidson introduced the K model, still a sidevalve and still displacing 750cc. It featured unit construction, a hand clutch and footshift four speed transmission. These things were already common on the British bikes with which it was intended to compete. The sidevalve 45 engine stayed in production to power the Servicar as detailed elsewhere in this book.

The saddlebags, screen and spotlights were all offered as official Harley-Davidson accessories and sold in Holland through dealers. Civilian Harleys went on sale immediately after World War II, but many people bought Army surplus machines

Above
Roel Donatz from Winterswijk restored this WLC, formerly used by the ANWB, and is seen here in the correct period costume to match the Liberator

Left
The huge toolbox mounted over the rear mudguard of the 45 was made from a recycled air supply container: an indication of how scarce metals were in Europe in the immediate postwar years

Right
Inside the toolbox were carried all the necessary tools and fluids to repair broken down cars by the side of the road. Also carried were flags to warn of obstructions

Above
These three-wheeler taxis, known as Tempos, appeared in India built from ex-military Harley-Davidsons. This Sikh-owned one is unusual in that it appears to have been constructed around a civilian 45. (Richard Rawsthorn)

Right
Pete Rigler is a member of the Harley-Davidson Riders' Club of Great Britain; he is seen here riding the 45 that he has owned for more than twenty years

Above
Although Pete Rigler has been riding this 45 for more than twenty years he has no plans to swap it for a newer one; he's happy with this sidevalve and the way it has evolved over the years

Left
Many of the original military components have been chrome plated over the years including the dash, handlebars and springers

Above

One of the longest trips Pete made on his 45 was in 1974 to Wolsztynie in Poland to a rally hosted by the Polish HD Club. He won a trophy for the longest distance travelled on a Harley to the rally

Left

Pete's 45 has gradually been civilianised and refined over the years – it was a chopper when he first bought it. It now has an Electra Glide seat and screen

Above

Ged Shorland is the owner of this 1947 WL that was originally sold in Canada. It was imported into Britain as a non-runner, something that the new owner soon put right

Left

In 1947 Harley-Davidson resumed full civilian production of motorcycles as materials became more freely available. In the postwar range was the WL – a more luxurious version of the motorcycle that had been supplied to the armies around the world

Above

For 1947 a new innovation was the use of a hydraulic damper on the springer forks, in place of the friction damper set-up used on prewar 45s

Left

Valanced mudguards, tombstone taillight, streamlined front sidelight, circular aircleaner, chrome plate and paint colours other than khaki are just some of the features that differentiate the postwar WLs from their wartime counterparts

Above

Sidecars were made by a variety of manufacturers and fitted to 45s; Goulding in the USA, Hollandia in Holland and Watsonian in the UK to name but three

Right

Since the earliest times, the 45 was intended to pull a sidecar. Machines with an 'S' in their designation were so designed and often had lower ratio gearing to enable them to pull the extra weight

Racing and Competition

Tom Sifton set up a Harley-Davidson dealership in San Francisco after some racing success in 1929. At the 1930 Pismo Beach Rally, a motocross-type event, Sifton entered on a 45. He rode with aired down tyres, twin downdraft carbs and brakes on both wheels. Sifton won, beating all the 80" stroke Indians and Harleys in the process. His future in competitive motorcycling was assured and he eventually retired from racing to concentrate on tuning.

The stock Indian Sport Scout had much less valve overlap (ie the time that both the inlet and exhaust valves are open together) than the stock Harley 45. Substantial valve overlap is found in racing engines because of the extreme speed ranges experienced. In touring engines the effectiveness of the 'porting' can be gauged by the amount of valve overlap required for all-round performance. The more valve overlap required for this all-round performance then the less effective is the shape of the ports and combustion chambers. The Sport Scout was a better breather than the stock Harley. By the late thirties the performance gap on the tracks had been closed, but not that on the roads. Sifton became known for his ability to make the Harley 45 run as fast as the Indian 45. He built bikes for his mechanic, Sam Arena, to race and a string of hill climb and flat track successes in California followed.

The 45 was to make its name as a racer in the USA in what became known as Class C. A man called E. C. Smith was the secretary of the American Motorcycle Association (AMA) in the early thirties. He was aware that racing was in decline and that the number of US motorcycle manufacturers was only two – namely Harley-Davidson and Indian. At that time motorcycle racing was roughly divided as follows: Hillclimbs – the professionals of Class A were limited to 45 cu in machines, and other than that there were few rules. All organisers needed to put on some good entertainment was a hill and some riders, so it was certain to attract an enthusiastic local crowd; Dirt Oval Racing – racers usually rode singles; Speedway – a type of racing imported from Europe; the tracks were mostly smaller than the dirt ovals and racers still rode mostly singles; TT

Harley 45s often grabbed the headlines in fierce competition with Indian. They used to race in Class C under the auspices of the American Motorcyclist Association. Times have changed but 45s still race, like this one at Daytona, with the American Historic Racing Motorcycle Association

Four sequential shots of Leo Anthony Junior in trouble at Daytona in 1993. Fortunately both rider and motorcycle lived to race another day

Racing – an early form of motocross with jumps, so speeds tended to be low. There were both 45 cu in and open classes. TT racing was named after the Isle of Man event and the rules required that courses had to include at least one right turn and one jump. Such courses were easier to build and maintain than the smooth flat tracks.

The AMA published the only surviving motorcycle magazine, *The Motorcyclist*, and in one of the 1933 issues, Smith called for significant changes to the structure of racing in the US. The existing Class A allowed for 21 cu in singles for circuit racing and 45 cu in twins for hillclimbing. Class B was for 45s and 80 inlet over exhaust engines for the semi-professional racers. Smith was keen to see a change as he felt that the existing race machinery was too expensive, thus deterring competitors and stifling development.

Class C was the resulting change; it debuted in the 1933 rulebooks but made more of an impression in 1934. Eventually Class C would bring both the Harley-Davidson and Indian factories back to the tracks. It aimed to attract those who were racing for sport, and they had to race on motorcycles that were the normal production ones that anyone could buy from a dealer. Homologation rules required that a minimum of 25 were produced. The rider must race on a machine that he owned and have the paperwork to prove it. The two factories both produced 45 cu in sidevalve V-twins in rigid frames with sprung forks when Class C was announced. Harley-Davidson had in its range the Model D 45, the DL – a higher compression version of the same machine and the sports version, and the DLD which boasted a larger carb. Class C events were organised for all types of motorcycle competition, hill climbs, flat tracks, TT and road races.

On July 15th 1934 at the Lakewood One mile dirt track, Harley-Davidsons had a 1 – 2 – 3 win in a 24-hour event. William Bracy and O. C. Hammond won on a 1933 45, having completed 1366 miles at an average of 57 mph. Bert Baisden and Todd Haygood covered 1359 miles on a 1934 bike for second place. In third were Jack Roberts and Harley Taylor who covered 1313 miles on a 1933 bike.

The first Daytona 200 was put on in 1937 with the blessing of the City of Daytona Beach. A 3.2 mile course was built incorporating two parallel 1.5 mile straights – one along the beach and the other along a paved road. The two were connected by sand turns. Ed Kretz won on an Indian, Clark Trumbull on a Norton took second and Ellis Pearce on a Harley 45 came in third. In 1938, for the second running of the event, there were 108 starters and victory eventually went to Ben Campanale from Rhode Island on a WLDR. Californian Sam Arena was in contention for the win until he crashed on the beach and was forced to retire because of the damage the sand did to his engine.

Arena did, however, win the 1938 Californian Oakland 200 when he cut

Above
The bike was repaired in time for the 1994 event; it's seen here with Leo Anthony (sitting) and Chet Dykgraaf. The Daytona 200 was still held on the beach when Leo finished 8th in 1949 and Chet 6th in 1940; both rode Harley 45s to these places

Right
The later WRs had a different timing case to allow for a magneto drive at the top of the cover. There was also an access plate at the front of the engine to allow access to the magneto drive to allow adjustment of the timing

19 minutes off the previous record. Sifton built an engine with a modified lubrication system that required the rider to hold the throttle open even through the turns of the dirt oval to prevent the plugs from fouling! This result proved that not only were Sifton's 45s fast, but that they were also reliable. He didn't drill con rods to achieve lightness or weaken other vital engine parts that might increase the chances of engine failure.

Campy, as the sleeves of Ben Campanale's racing jersey read, repeated his Daytona victory in 1939. The first Daytona 200s were essentially clashes between the Indian and Harley factories although such diverse brands as Norton, Ariel and BMW are listed in the top twenty placings. So it was for 1940 when Babe Tancrede, another Rhode Islander, and riding a WLDR took the chequered flag after a battle with Jimmy Kelly, a Californian, on an Indian 45. Campanale (HD), Arena (HD) and Kretz (Indian) all had to retire due to mechanical problems. This year there were 15 Harley-Davidsons, three Indians and two British makes – Norton and Triumph – in the top twenty. The pattern followed for 1941 except

Above
Race engines, especially old ones, need building to a high standard if they're to go the distance. Jim Lucas of Moon Lite Cycles built this WLDD engine for Al Perry

Left
Al Perry restored and races this 1939 WLDD with sponsorship from Suffolk County HD, David Sarafan Inc and Perry Brothers Racing

that Canadian Billy Mathews on a Norton won. Previous winners Tancrede and Camapanale, both members of the Rhode Island Ramblers MC, finished in 2nd and 4th places respectively. In the top twenty were 16 Harleys, 3 Indians and the winning Norton.

The 1939 Oakland 200 was held on October 1st and WLDRs took the first two places. Jack Cotterill won, having averaged 82.28 mph, and Armando Magri, placed second.

Sifton built two engines for the 1940 Oakland 200, one for Arena and one for Gus Hunter. Sadly Gus Hunter was killed in a crash while practising that also completely destroyed the bike.

Sifton built another engine for Louis Guanella who won averaging 84.64 mph. This was a record for a long distance event because, although the speeds for shorter events were greater, it was generally acknowledged that the sidevalves got slower as they ran. Sifton's engines were actually

Al Knapp, a veteran racer, competes in AHRMA events on this 1940 WLDR. The engine runs a Wico magneto which was originally designed for agricultural tractor applications!

Although the race plate 883 may give the impression that we're talking Sportsters here, it's actually a 45 cu in WR out on Daytona's famous track

running as fast in the last laps as they were in the first.

Tom Sifton knew that the majority of the exhaust valve heat had to be transmitted away through the valve seats. The eccentric layout of the sidevalve design caused a particular problem because the valves were heated unevenly. This resulted in uneven expansion – the side closest to the cylinder bore became hotter and therefore expanded more. An out of round condition ensued which prevented the valves from seating properly. This exacerbated the warping problem by conducting even less heat away through the valve seats, and accounted for the loss of power in long races. One of Sifton's ideas for solving this problem was to use rotating valve lifters made from modified truck components. In 1941 he experimented with the valves and porting of the 45 sidevalve. He fitted oversize inlet valves and found that, somewhat unexpectedly, power was reduced. Thinking it may be because of the increased weight of the larger valves

Left
After World War Two, racing resumed on bikes that were little changed from the prewar machines. No. 546 is a 1947 WR 45

Right
The WR had larger valves than a standard WL. They were inclined towards the cylinder bores to ease the flow of inlet and exhaust gases. WR engines also had lighter tappets and flywheel assembly

he machined up some lightweight ones and tried these. They made no difference, so he thought again. He cast up plaster of Paris moulds of the insides of the cylinder heads. He then took a section through the mould between the valve pocket and the volume of the bore. On measuring the area of this cross-section he discovered that it was 30% smaller than the area surrounding the intake valve port when the valve was fully open. Not afraid to question tuning convention and accepted theories, he figured that compression ratio and squish effect had been taken too far for performance purposes. Therefore the engine wasn't breathing as effectively as it should. To remedy the problem Sifton machined a channel in the cylinder block which had the effect of enlarging the combustion chamber. The results of this experiment were phenomenal and increased torque throughout the rev range, which was also increased as the engine would now rev higher. This unorthodox approach was a winner and the Arena and Sifton team raced and won on half and quarter mile tracks in the immediate postwar period. After considerable success Sifton retired temporarily from racing.

The Harley factory introduced the WR – a production racer that conformed to Class C regulations – in 1941. It came from the racing department which was under the direction of Hank Syvertson. The racing department built bikes for customers, assisted other racers and sometimes even lent out race bikes. One reason for the introduction of such racers was because the Indian Sport Scout was lighter and faster than the WLD and Indian's Ed Kretz was winning a lot of races. The company were looking for a fourth successive win at Daytona and had high hopes for the

WRTT. Because there were two types of racing there were two WR variants – the WR and WRTT. They were the first Harley-Davidsons equipped solely as Class C racers.

The WR came without front brakes for flat track racing. It had a different frame, the castings were the same but the frame tubes were made from chrome molybdenum tubing which was stronger and lighter than the mild steel of the WL frames.

The WRTT came without lights and with cut down front and rear mudguards. It used a WL frame with the lugs ground off (there were some special chrome molybdenum ones), the seat was solid on a sprung seat post and used the WL clutch and brake pedals.

The WLDR became the road model with lights but hot cams and was claimed to rev to 5500 and had 7 hp more than the WLD. In 1939 the WLDR became known as the WLDD. The factory offered WL owners a tuning kit to convert their road bikes into racers. The kit included cylinders, heads, cams, tappets and an intake manifold for $109. Exhausts and a carburettor were extra.

The WRTT and WR had a 1.75" diameter crankpin and conrod assembly. They had special intake and exhaust cam gears, a 1.5" carburettor and 25% stronger valve springs. Polished intake ports, manifold and combustion chamber eased the induction. The WRTT and WR had the same tuned engine which included lighter flat tappets in place of the roller tappets fitted to other engines. The WR barrel had larger valves set closer to the cylinder and inclined towards the bore in

Above

The WLDR was originally Harley's racer but after the introduction of the WR it became the 'sports' road model with performance camshafts. It would rev to 5500 rpm

Left

Most 45 sidevalves used for racing utilise a magneto. In postwar years both Edison Splitdorf and Wico components were available for 45s, this WLDR has been fitted with a Hunt Magneto

order to straighten the path taken by the inlet and exhaust gases. The inclined valves meant that 'shoes' had to be fitted to square the valves to the cams. The engines used paint in place of a head gasket. WR engines didn't have generators; originally they came with an Edison Splitdorf magneto horizontally mounted where the generator would normally be. The 1947 WR stayed pretty much the same as the 1941 model but from 1948 onwards a Wico magneto was available. The Wico magneto was originally designed for agricultural tractor applications and was mounted vertically. Later, customers had a choice of either a vertically or horizontally mounted Wico.

To race these bikes the AMA allowed some changes to be made to their specification, even though they were meant to be showroom stock for Class C. Competitors, they were allowed a choice of either 18 or 19" wheels with 3.25 or 4.00" tyres and a variety of petrol and oil tanks. The WR had a dual tank with petrol on the left and oil on the right. The WRTT for longer events had a dual tank with both halves containing 2.5 gallons each of petrol. The oil was stored in an oil tank under the seat – this set up was referred to as 'Daytona Tanks'. The WR primary chain had a 0.375" pitch while the WRTT had the option of 0.5" for long races.

Sadly the WR didn't bring Harley victory at Daytona, either before or after the war, and a win there wouldn't be Harley's until 1953. Racing at Daytona was suspended for the duration of the war. It resumed in 1947 in much the same format and with the same machines that had been used up until 1941. The only noticeable change was the appearance of greater numbers of British 500cc motorcycles (the rules for Class C permitted 750cc sidevalves and 500cc overhead valves to compete), especially Nortons and Triumphs. The footclutch/handshift American motorcycles were starting to look antique when compared to the British bikes, but that's not to say that they weren't racing. In 1947 there were fourteen Harley-Davidson 45s in the top 20. In 1948 there were eight, then nine in 1949, and 10 in 1950. The number fell to six in 1951 and three in 1952. A lack of wins forced the Milwaukee concern back to the drawing board to replace the now obsolete WR. The result was the KR which Michigan rider Paul Goldsmith took to victory in 1953, the first year it was entered.

National Class A hillclimbs were held at Mount Garfield near Muskegon, Michigan in 1946. Harley-Davidson's C. W. Hemmins beat Indian's Jimmy Raspach in the 45 cu in Class when he climbed a 360 feet slope in 7.91 seconds. Class C hillclimbs were held a week later. Hemmins beat Indian's Brownie Baker.

The lure of racing proved too strong for Tom Sifton to stay away from for long, and in 1950 he was back at the tracks. He teamed up with the Expert Class rider, Larry Headrick and they contested events on mile tracks. Headrick won the 15 mile National in Milwaukee and then the

Springfield, Illinois 25 mile National and the AMA No.1 Plate for the 1951 season. Larry Headrick had a motorcycle accident while riding on the street and gave up racing. In 1951 Sifton worked with another Expert Class rider, Kenny Eggers, and an amateur, Joe Leonard. Yet again Sifton's engines brought success to the riders, and Tom Sifton let the Milwaukee factory in on some of his secrets. He passed his dealership on to Sam Arena and went on to build race engines full time for Joe Leonard who had graduated into the Expert Class. Sifton and Leonard turned their attention to the new K models with great success.

A different type of motorcycle competition altogether was the Endurance Run, which can be compared to a reliability trial. In 1930 Bill Davidson, the son of the Vice President and Works Manager William Davidson, entered the Jack Pine Tour organised by The Lansing Motorcycle Club. This two-day event was nicknamed The Cow Bell Classic because the winner's name was inscribed on an old cowbell. Davidson entered on a stock 1930 45 and rode the 420 gruelling miles around northern Michigan, some cross country and a lot on unsurfaced tracks, and won the Class A solo event. By 1941 Harley-Davidson mounted riders had won the Jack Pine Endurance Run for the 17th time in a row.

The Los Angeles to New York City record belonged to Indian when in 1934 Randolph Whiting set a record of 4 days 19 hours on one. On September 19th of that year, Earl Robinson from Saginaw, Michigan, on a 1935 RLD set a new record of 77 hours 53 minutes for the 3005 miles. It only stood until the following spring when the well known Indian rider, Rody Rodenburg, set a time of 2 days 23 hours.

Race number 44J is a 1948 WR, the brace at the rear of the frame, the sprung solo saddle and the fact that the bike has no front brake can be clearly seen.

The Servicar

In 1931 Indian Motorcycles offered the three-wheeler Dispatch Tow – a 101 Scout low compression engine with two rear wheels on a differential equipped axle with a box body over it. A yoke-type attachment was fitted to the front with a clamp for attaching to automobile rear bumpers. Around 400 were sold in the first season. The idea was highly regarded and Harley-Davidson offered one soon after. They wheeled out the Servicar – a 45 flathead powered three-wheeler with a large load-carrying capacity designed for commercial users – on 9th November 1931 for the 1932 sales season. It retailed at $450. It would stay in production, albeit with various improvements and updates, until 1973.

The purpose of the Servicar was as a local delivery truck for small businesses, as a parking ticket dispenser for Police Departments, and as a service truck for garages who had use the Servicar as a means of dispatching a mechanic to breakdowns. The metal box on the rear was suitable for signwriting and the Servicar was regarded as quite a different product to the company's sidecar outfits.

Throughout its long production run most of the Servicar updates ran hand-in-hand with the development of the 45 sidevalve solos. In 1933 there was a choice of either large or small body, but for '34 there were four variants: large or small body, with or without tow bar and a combination rear bumper and spare tyre carrier. Still deep in the Depression, advertising for 1934 made much of the economy angle, 'Servicar will handle 500 lb loads at a fraction the cost of light trucks or autos'. For '35 there was a new constant mesh transmission for solos and trikes, as well as improved brakes and a beefed-up rear axle on threes. Like the Indian Dispatch Tow the Servicar axle, on all models, was chain driven through a differential. The commercial uses to which Servicars were mostly put meant compliance with different state laws – such as the requirement in 1936 to fit an auxiliary towbar safety cable. Taste, meantime, dictated the change to a chromed rear body latch. A fold-up towbar fitted to the front axle was requested by users, and this allowed garage users to drive out to collect a customer's car and return to the garage towing the Servicar.

Harley-Davidson introduced the Servicar in 1931; it was aimed at commercial users such as despatch companies and garages. This is a 1934 model and has I-section forks. Most of the Servicar updates ran parallel to those made to 45 solo models

For 1937 the Servicar underwent something of a restyle, with an apron extending from the front bottom edge of the seat box to the seat post. Larger hubcaps were fitted as were individual rear brakes. Changes continued into the '38 model year with a larger and presumably more effective silencer, the drive chain was enclosed and a new style of towbar was made available. The towbar set-up for garage Servicars was permanently attached to the front end to save space in the rear box and to save operators the effort of attaching and detaching it between jobs – it didn't do much for the appearance of the machine though! Detail changes were made to the size of Servicar bodies and trim parts adorning them.

The 1940 Servicars saw a myriad of detail changes. The rear axle case was strengthened further with an increased thickness of metal around the chain opening to reduce the likelihood of damage in the event of a chain snapping. The clearance of the chainguard was increased to reduce noise

Above

The Model G Servicar for 1937 had been slightly redesigned but retained the iron cylinder heads with 4.5:1 compression ratio. The chrome handles fitted to the cargo box were an official accessory

Right

Lieke Hessels owns this 1937 model G Servicar which she and her husband restored over a three year period. They purchased it in parts from an autojumble

from the chain striking the guard. The rear brakes were redesigned, with cast drums being introduced and a simplified method of brake adjustment. The battery box was moved to give more room for the clutch arm.

The Servicar brochure for 1940 enthused about the convenience of the three-wheelers for use by garage proprietors, and drew attention to the three models then available – the G, GE and GDT. The latter had an extra large capacity body. A model line-up for 1941 was announced and again included a number of changes to the Servicar specification. The compression ratio was upped from 4.5:1 to 4.75:1 and a number of improvements were made to the clutch – generally beefing it up and smoothing its action. Up front the big twin front wheel and front brake were fitted for improved braking. Following Harley's pattern of announcing 'next year's models' in the autumn of the previous year, a 1942 model line up was announced – though civilian production was cut right back to essential sales once military contracts for solos were awarded. The '42 line up discontinued the smallest of the Servicar bodies.

During World War II, and in line with Harley-Davidson's military business and US Quartermaster Corps specifications, the company toyed with the idea of a military shaft drive Servicar and eventually submitted a bid. Despite this move they attempted to persuade the army to accept chain drive trikes. The upshot was a contract to build sixteen Knucklehead trikes with shaft drive and solid disc wheels. The shaft drive design necessitated bevel gears, which Harley were intent on having made by subcontractors. A prototype was sent to the US Army test base at Camp

Holabird – with disappointing results. Vibration, oil leaks, a tail-heavy weight distribution and odd handling characteristics all added up to the need for a re-think. A second prototype was delivered to the US Army in August 1940, and after more successful tests, received cautious approval.

Harley-Davidson went ahead and started work on the remaining fifteen trikes in the contract. Shaft drive wasn't forgotten by the US Army who continued their interest in shaft drive solos – but once the Willys Jeep had been proven a success, in 1941, they soon lost interest in three-wheelers.

Postwar, Harley planned the Model K Servicar – a shaft drive, horizontally opposed twin powered variant, but it never went further than the prototype stage. Instead, post war production of the Servicar continued as before with numerous detail improvements through the years. For example, a new design of dash in 1947 followed by a redesigned front mudguard in 1948. In the official 1947 Accessory Catalogue, as well as accessories that would fit all Harleys, there were numerous items exclusive to the Servicar including a seat cushion and handrails for the top of the load box. For $15.75 the Servicar owner could buy a complete seat and handrail assembly for all 1933-47 GD and GDT models. A similar package was available for 1939-41 G and GA Servicars; such accessories were of course useful in that they allowed the Servicar to carry a passenger. For an extra $7, a rear bumper, part number 13005-X was available to fit all Servicars. The design of the Servicar occasionally necessitated exclusive special tools and these too were listed in the catalogue; part number 12072-37 Servicar Wheel Puller 1937-47 models, $8.

Something that was useful for commercial Servicar users were 'fender ad skirts'. These were semi-circular metal panels that fitted the inside edge of the Servicar's rear mudguards and were designed to be signwritten with the user's business name and telephone number. They were supplied in either stock Harley-Davidson colours or in primer for owners who used Servicars in their business livery. To assist the garage owners who used Servicars for collecting and returning customers' cars, batches of leaflet folders were available, printed by Harley-Davidson. These read, 'We collect your car', showed pictures of a Servicar, and emphasised the convenience of the service. Sufficient space was left to overprint the dealer's name and address. In 1947 100 postcard size folders were 75 cents.

Harley clearly saw their Servicar as important for traffic control in urban areas. In 1949 an advert aimed specifically at those who managed parking meters stated that a Servicar 'speeds meter servicing' and went on to point out the advantages of using a Servicar for meter emptying, dispensing parking tickets and controlling traffic. In 1951 hydraulic brakes and solid steel wheels were fitted to the Servicar. When the 45 cubic inch solo models were discontinued in 1952 the sidevalve engine was kept in production as the powerplant for Servicars.

Above
The 1942 line up were the last civilian machines produced prior to America becoming actively involved in World War II. Also in this year the smallest size of load box was discontinued

Right
Many of the accessories Harley-Davidson made for their solos were equally suitable for Servicars; examples are the front crashbar, spotlight bar and spotlights fitted to this GE model

The Servicar was also sold with specialist commercial applications in mind such as refrigerated bodies for ice cream sales, water spraying equipment and white line painting machines.

For 1953 Harley advertised new brighter colours. A note to dealers from the factory pointed out that the rapid expansion of urban areas meant that Police Departments required more machines for meter servicing, parking ticket dispensing and suchlike. It urged them to actively 'sell' the Servicars to their local Police Departments.

In 1958 the springer forks were replaced with the hydraulic ones, as fitted to the Hydraglide. For 1964 the Servicar was the first H-D product to be fitted with an electric start, a year prior to the announcement of the 74 cu in Electra Glide. Following on from this, in 1966, the dynamo was dropped in favour of an alternator to handle the extra load of starting the sidevalve engine. The alternator was mounted on the downtube of the frame and partially concealed in a pressed metal cover that was painted to match the petrol tank and mudguards.

Modern materials caught up with the Servicar in 1967 when the load box was manufactured in glassfibre. AMF (American Machine and Foundry) took over the management of H-D in 1969 and still the Servicar continued. In 1973, the last year of the production run, AMF saw fit to install the big twin disc brake up front.

John Hessels owns this 1955 GE Servicar. When he purchased it, it had several layers of paint on it. As it was stripped down he discovered the logo of the Semo Motor Patrol on the original red paint. When the restoration was complete it was repainted exactly as the original

Left

The Servicar used the big-twin Harley front forks with slightly heavier rockers on the forks than on the solos and a big twin drum brake. By 1955 the mudguard was also the same as the big twin, as the solo 45s had been discontinued in 1952

Above

The load-carrying ability of the Servicar made it suitable for numerous commercial applications. This one has been adapted for water spraying and is seen here damping down the dust in an American suburb during the fifties. (National Motor Museum)

Above
Many US Police departments used Servicars for a variety of traffic control duties ranging from emptying parking meters to dispensing parking tickets. This machine from the late forties has wire spoked wheels all round and is equipped with a radio. (National Motor Museum)

Right
Although the Servicar was included in the Dutch sales brochures for Harley-Davidson, they are not known to have sold any – which is why both the Hessels' and Elly Donders' machines were imported secondhand from the USA

Above
A particular use to which Servicars were put was as ice cream floats. This one was still dispensing lollies and cornets in 1994 at The Volusia County Fairgrounds outside Daytona

Right
Solid steel rear wheels and hydraulic brakes first appeared on the Servicar in 1951. This particular three-wheeler is probably ex-Police Department and is seen here at a Daytona swapmeet

Above
The chain driven rear axle in a triangular frame easily lends itself to modification – this custom trike seen in New Mexico is based on a post-'64 Servicar

Left
The Hydraglide front end was fitted to the Servicar in 1958 replacing the springer forks that had been fitted since 1931

Modern Times

The film 'Easy Rider' was released in 1969 and influenced a whole generation. Motorcyclists everywhere wanted choppers. In Europe, the only plentiful Harleys were the war surplus 45s, and these became the basis for many early choppers. In London, Ray Leon and John Wallace built Harley 45 choppers in a shop on Putney Bridge Road. It was the same in other countries – in France, for example, Brigitte Bardot had a 45 chop that she recorded a song about. A common trick for those building 45 chops was to mate the engine up to a British gearbox such as those in pre-unit Triumphs and BSAs. This had the effect of giving both a four speed gearbox and a foot gearchange. In those days the 45 was still plentiful and not particularly desirable, something that has changed in recent years. The growing popularity of Harley-Davidsons worldwide has increased the interest in, and values of, the bikes that survived the Depression and won the War. Around the world there are dealers who specialise in parts for 45s – Jan Willem Boon in Holland, Tony Bairstow in London, David Sarafan in Albuquerque, New Mexico and The 45 Restoration Co in Albany, New York to name but four.

As a result, it is not uncommon to see restored WLA and WLC Army bikes on show at both military vehicle and classic motorcycle events. Civilian and military 45s are welcomed by both the classic fraternity and the newer, younger Harley-Davidson aficionados. At a custom show on either side of the Atlantic it is still likely that there will be at least one 45 powered chopper or trike. The Servicar's mechanical configuration easily lends itself to becoming the basis for any number of wild custom trikes. Because of the long production run of the 45 in the various guises there is a huge selection of related ephemera and militaria to collect.

The humble Harley-Davidson 45 has even been the star of a movie. 'Born to Ride', was released in 1991 by Warner Brothers, a Fred Weintraub/Incovent Production and a Graham Baker Film. It starred John Stamos, John Stockwell and Teri Polo. The film concerns some American soldiers in a mission to rescue a scientist from the Nazis in Spain before World War II! It has an implausible storyline and contains some rewriting of history in terms of dates of historical incidents, and is also careless in

Tall, skinny front wheel, wider smaller rear wheel, 'bobbed' rear mudguard, flame paint and apehangers, this 45 is '50s period perfect chopper. It may come as a surprise to learn that is was built not in America, but in Britain by Steve Studd

Left

Flathead Phil, who owns this bike, looks as though he's just stepped out of 'The Loveless' – one of the classic biker films set in the early sixties

Above

Another early-style chopper is this Bobjob, photographed in the American sunshine. The Johnny Kool motif on the oil tank is typical of the fifties too!

matters such as the neutrality of certain countries. Despite all this, and in the best tradition of motion pictures, it is entertaining if only for the numbers of 45s and exciting riding sequences. Some of the stunts were done by Jim Dowdall a noted Harley 45 and XA enthusiast. One of the songs in the movie is 'Born to be Wild' – the theme song of the infinitely more famous bike movie, 'Easy Rider'.

In Australia, where WLAs are known as 'Wallas', a group of owners celebrated the fiftieth anniversary of the model with a weekend rally. It has now become an annual event. In Britain, an owners' club exclusively for Harley 45s has been formed and is going from strength to strength. It is still easy to buy t-shirts that proclaim the 45 as, 'the bike that won the war'. There are plenty of miles left in Harley's 45 yet.

Above

Glen Joliffe built this bike towards the end of the seventies. It is typical of the era with extended springer forks, a rigid frame, a small petrol tank and metalflake paintjob. (Phil Mather)

Left

A completely different style of chopper appeared in the seventies, clearly inspired by the bikes that starred in 'Easy Rider'. Ray Leon and John Wallace built this bike in the early seventies. (Phil Mather)

Above

*Long forked 45 chops haven't gone out
of fashion. Prof from Dorset, England,
built this one with a Triumph frame
over the last few years after buying a
secondhand engine*

Left

*The Harley engine has been mated to a
Triumph four speed gearbox. This, of
course, changes the gearing completely
and allows the use of a foot gearchange.
Over the gearbox is the oil tank*

Right

*The long forks of a chopper on the
road add to an evocative image – one
that is as valid today as in 1969 when
'Easy Rider' was first screened*

Above

A BSA M20 rigid frame holds the 45 engine and the BSA gearbox of Dave Morris's flat track style bike. The oil tank is under the seat; a Sportster tank holds the petrol

Left

The BSA primary cover looks as though it was made for the job, while the forks are from a Norton. A sprung solo seat, wide handlebars and a single instrument add to the impression of an early dirt bike

Above

The author's 45 chop under construction. It is possible to see the mix and match of parts that goes into such a bike. Suzuki forks, Sportster tank, Suzuki front wheel, Harley rear wheel as well as a modified rear mudguard and custom sidepanels are just some of the parts. Most chops and specials use a similar mixture of components

Right

Many 45s, of course, still exist and are ridden in completely stock form. An example is this WL in New Mexico for the 1993 Vietnam Veterans MC annual memorial run to Red River

Above

The modifications made to 45s often tend towards the cosmetic, such as this bike belonging to Brian Rooney. He has brass plated many of the parts and painted the bike a sympathetic colour

Above right

Servicars, too, are regularly street ridden – as often by women as men. This fifties survivor was photographed on the 1993 Red River Run in New Mexico

Right

A stripped down Servicar with extended forks and wide back wheels is just the thing for riding in the Sturgis sunshine

Above

Although this Servicar looks as though it has been extensively modified, it is actually fairly standard. The cargo box has been removed, longer forks have been fitted and the headstock has been altered to allow them to fit. A custom seat is fitted and a number of other smaller modifications have been made, all adding up to a neat trike

Above right

Jose and Sandra Boon inside Jan Willem Boon's 45 Shop. The Naaldwijk premises near Rotterdam, Holland are a veritable Aladdin's Cave of 45 parts

Right

Max Middelbosch runs a Museum of old American motorcycles in Zwolle, Holland. He has purchased machines all around the world and is seen here sitting behind the WL 45s he races

Specifications

Model DL

Year 1930
Engine sidevalve v-twin
Displacement 45.12 cu in
Bore and stroke 2.75 x 3.8125"
Horsepower 18.5 bhp @ 4000 rpm
Compression ratio 5.0:1
Gearbox 3 speed
Wheelbase 57.5"
Weight 390 lbs
Top Speed 65 mph

Model WR

Year 1941
Engine sidevalve V-twin
Displacement 45.12 cu in
Bore and stroke 2.75 x 3.8125"
Horsepower 38 bhp
Compression ratio n/a
Gearbox 3 speed
Wheelbase 57.5"
Weight n/a
Top Speed n/a

Model WLC

Year 1941
Engine sidevalve V-twin
Displacement 45.12 cu in
Bore and stroke 2.75 x 3.8125"
Horsepower 23 bhp
Compression ratio 5.0:1
Gearbox 3 speed
Wheelbase 57.5"
Weight 576 lbs
Top Speed 65 mph

Model XA

Year 1942
Engine sidevalve Horizontally opposed twin
Displacement 45.038 cu in
Bore and stroke 3.125 x 3.125"
Horsepower 23 bhp @ 4600 rpm
Compression ratio 5.7:1
Gearbox four speed
Wheelbase 58.75"
Weight 538 lbs
Top Speed n/a

Model WLA

Year 1942
Engine sidevalve V-twin
Displacement 45.12 cu in
Bore and stroke 2.75 x 3.8125"
Horsepower 23 bhp @4600 rpm
Compression ratio 5.0:1
Gearbox 3 speed
Wheelbase 57.5"
Weight 576 lbs
Top Speed 65 mph

Model G

Year 1950
Engine sidevalve V-twin
Displacement 45.12 cu in
Bore and stroke 2.75 x 3.8125"
Horsepower 23 bhp @ 4600 rpm
Compression ratio 4.75:1
Gearbox 3 speed
Wheelbase 61.5"
Weight 1395 lbs
Top Speed 50 mph